Published in the United States of America in 1991
by Universe
300 Park Avenue South, New York, NY 10010

© 1991 Tom Robb

91 92 93 94 95 / 10 9 8 7 6 5 4 3 2 1

Library of Congress Catalog Card Number: 91–18764

ISBN: 0–87663–619–9

Printed in Germany

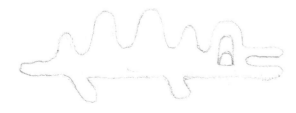  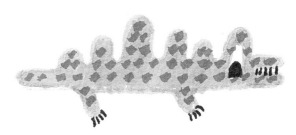

TOM ROBB

FIRST STEPS IN PAINT

A new and simple way to learn
how to paint step by step

UNIVERSE

1 What You Will Need

A set of watercolor paints usually comes in a paint box with round pans of eight basic colors. The best paint boxes have a lid where you can mix colors, and deep pans of paint. Very shallow pans may not hold enough paint to make rich, bright colors.

If your paint box does not have a lid, or you have tubes of paint, use an old white saucer or plate for mixing. Keep the plate clean by rinsing it with water after you have mixed three or four colors. Otherwise the colors will run into each other and look muddy.

You will need two brushes – a thin brush for details like birds' eyes and feathers, and a thick brush for painting larger shapes, as well as the sky, the grass, the background, and so on. Look after your brushes carefully. If you leave them in water, with the brush end down, the hairs will stick out at the sides and you won't be able to paint fine lines or little details.

A sketch pad of good watercolor paper is best to paint on. Shiny paper is no good – the paint just slides and runs all over it.

You will also need a pencil, an eraser and a pencil sharpener. Use the pencil to draw outlines very lightly before you start to paint – then you are sure there will be enough room for the whole picture.

Don't forget the glass of water.

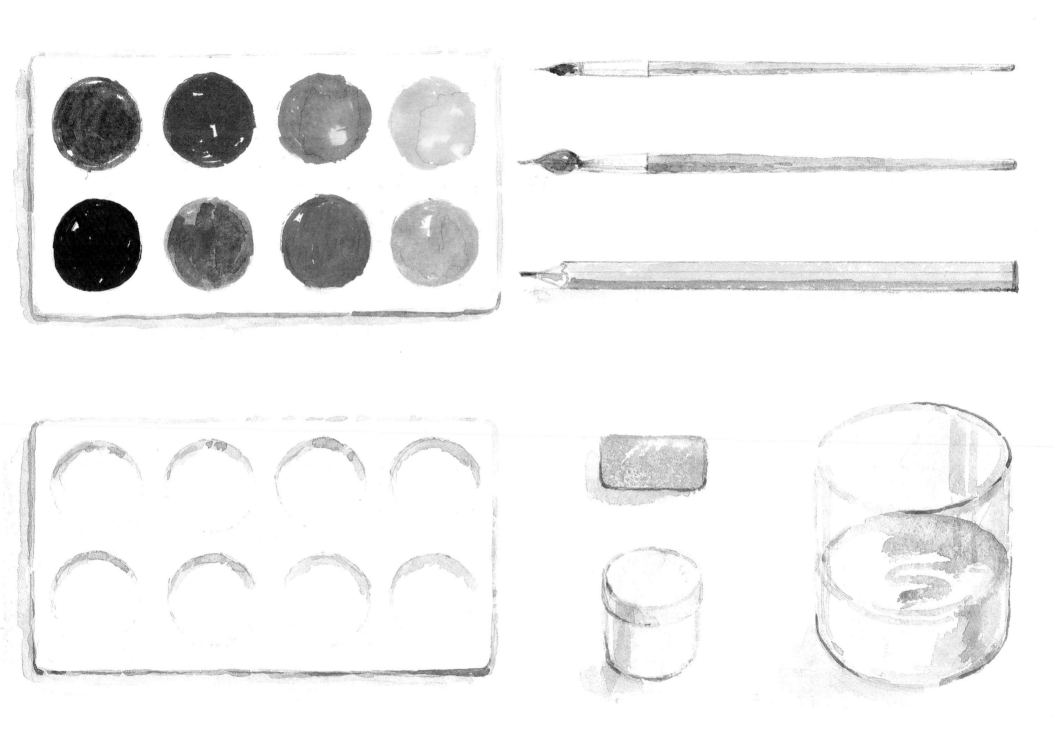

2 Holding Your Brush

A brush is not just for big sloshy colors. It is also for neat lines and small parts of the picture.

FIRST STEPS

Practice holding a brush as if it were a pencil. Dip it gently into the water, then press it very lightly against the edge of the glass, so the extra water drips back into the glass. Never push the brush down hard into the water, or onto the paint.

Put the wet brush on the paint you want. Rub gently in a circular motion. Lift the brush and the liquid paint onto your mixing plate, or onto one of the hollows in the lid of your paint box.

Paint on a bit of scrap paper to see what the color looks like. If it is too light, add a little more paint. If it is too dark, add a little clean water. Try it again. When you think the color is just right, you're ready to start painting.

SECOND STEPS

Draw a flower shape with the pencil. Don't press hard – you may want to erase any lines that go wrong.

Start painting one of the petals with the thick brush. Paint all around the edge, then fill in the center. Do each petal in turn until the flower is finished. Paint some thin lines and dots with the small brush. Practice with both brushes.

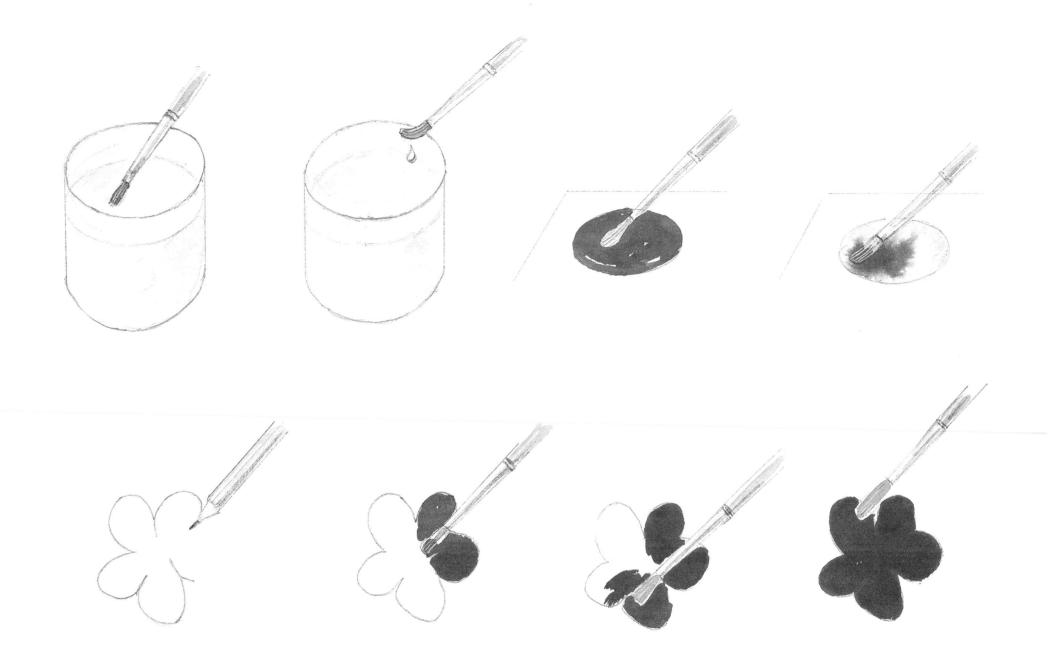

3 Mixing Colors

It's fun to mix colors together to make your own special effects.

Never put one color directly onto another color in the paint box. Lift each color separately with the brush onto a clean mixing space. Rinse the brush clean in water, then add another color a drop at a time. Twirl the brush gently until the colors are blended.

Always start with the light color, and add the darker color drop by drop. Remember to rinse out your brush every time you go back to another color.

Make a chart like this to remind you:

Start with yellow, add a drop of blue and it makes green.

Start with red, add a drop of blue and it makes lilac.

Start with yellow, add a drop of red and it makes orange.

Rinse off the lid or saucer when you have finished painting for the day. You will then be ready to mix new colors the next time you settle down to paint.

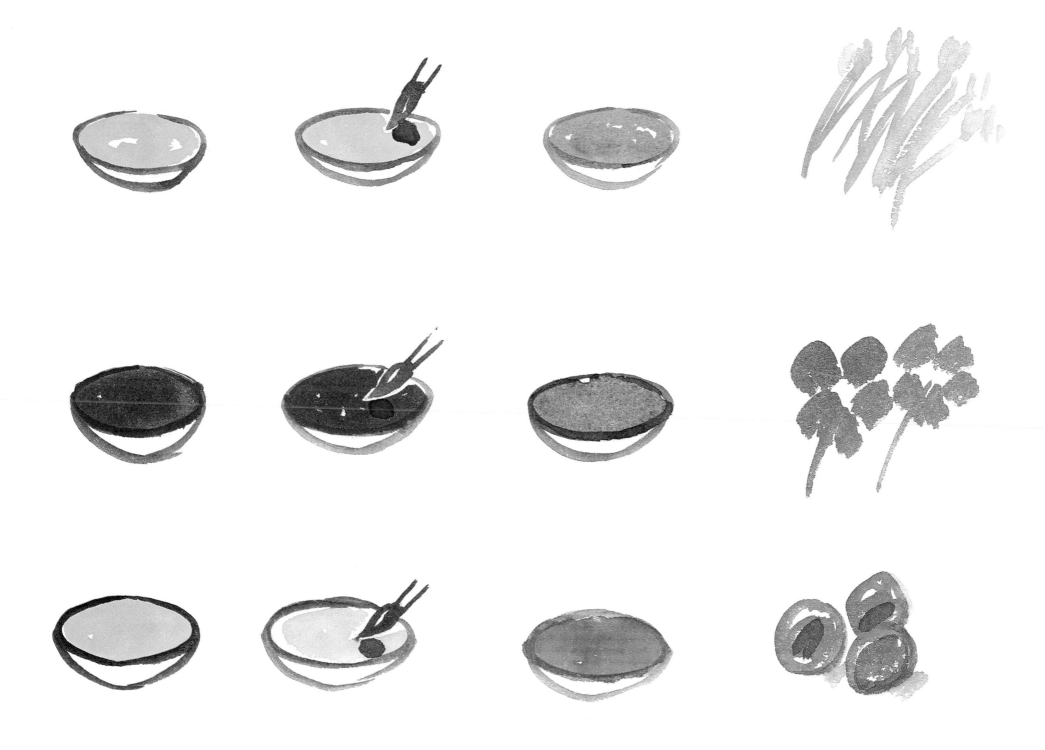

4 Spiraling Snails

Here's a very simple shape to start with. The snail's house travels with him. It's the biggest part of him too.

FIRST STEPS

Use the thick brush to paint a simple circle, but leave a gap for the snail's head and body. You can make this first circle any color you like. If you paint it with a light color, the spiral will stand out better.

Wait for the circle to be completely dry before you put in the spiral. Touch it gently with your finger to make sure – it only takes a minute.

Now paint the spiral. You can use the same color with more paint to make it darker, or you can rinse out your brush and use a new color.

SECOND STEPS

Paint the snail's head and body with just a few strokes, still using the thick brush. When the paint is completely dry, use the thin brush and a darker color to paint his smiling mouth, eye and two antennae. Now add a wavy line for him to crawl along!

5   Splotches and Strokes

Look what you can do with just a few splotches and strokes!

FIRST STEPS

Everyone loves dinosaurs, so here's one to start with. Paint a half-circle, then add the head with one wavy stroke. Add a row of straight spines along his back, an eye, two feet, and maybe an ear.

SECOND STEPS

A slowpoke of a turtle begins with a simple oval of green. Add four brown strokes for his feet, two for his head and tail, and two eyes.

THIRD STEPS

Here's how to make paint look spiky. Make lots of little strokes close together for the hedgehog's spines. Then all you need are four feet and a sharp nose.

You can paint the turtle and the hedgehog having a race – who will win?

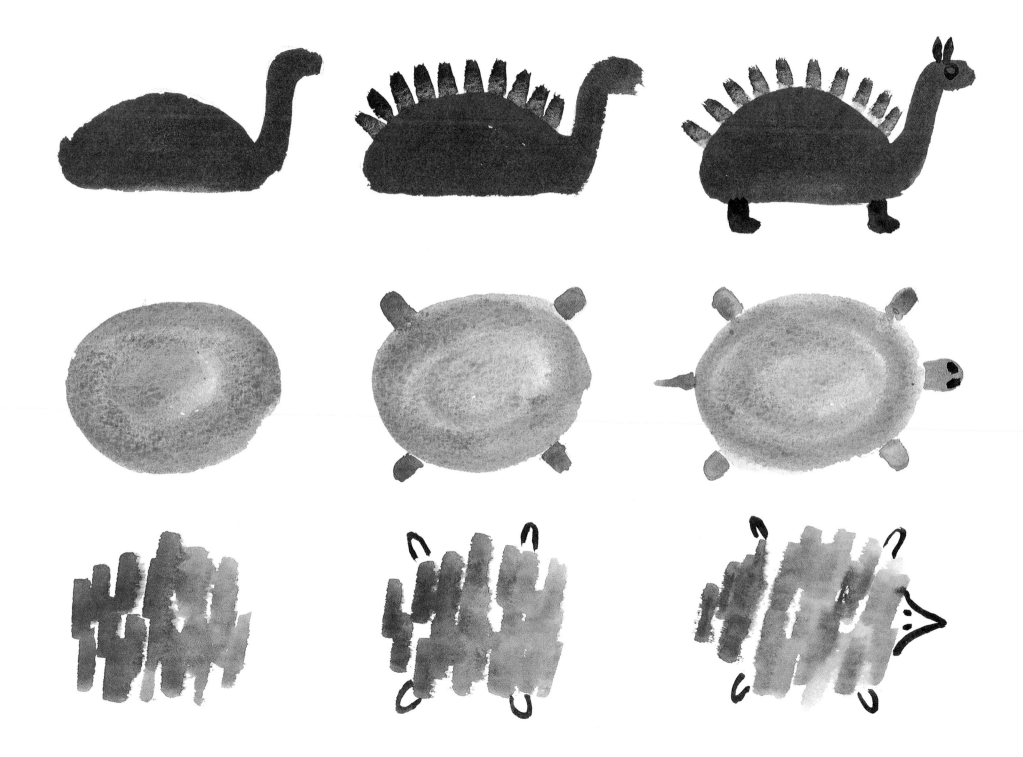

6 Squiggles and Lines

Once you can make splotches and strokes, it's time to try squiggles and lines.

FIRST STEPS

Start with a round stroke as if you were going to paint a circle. A little flick at the end makes a tail. Add a curvy line on the bottom, and a few more for the markings on the side. An eye and a smile, and your fish is ready to swim away!

Remember to wash out the brush in the glass each time you pick up a new color.

SECOND STEPS

Paint a wavy line with the thick brush. Add a few dots, a tiny eye and a forked tongue, and it's clearly a snake in the grass!

THIRD STEPS

Start with a simple oval painted with the thick brush. Add a smaller oval for the head. A few blobs make front and back feet, two ears and a tail – and you have the carrot's best friend!

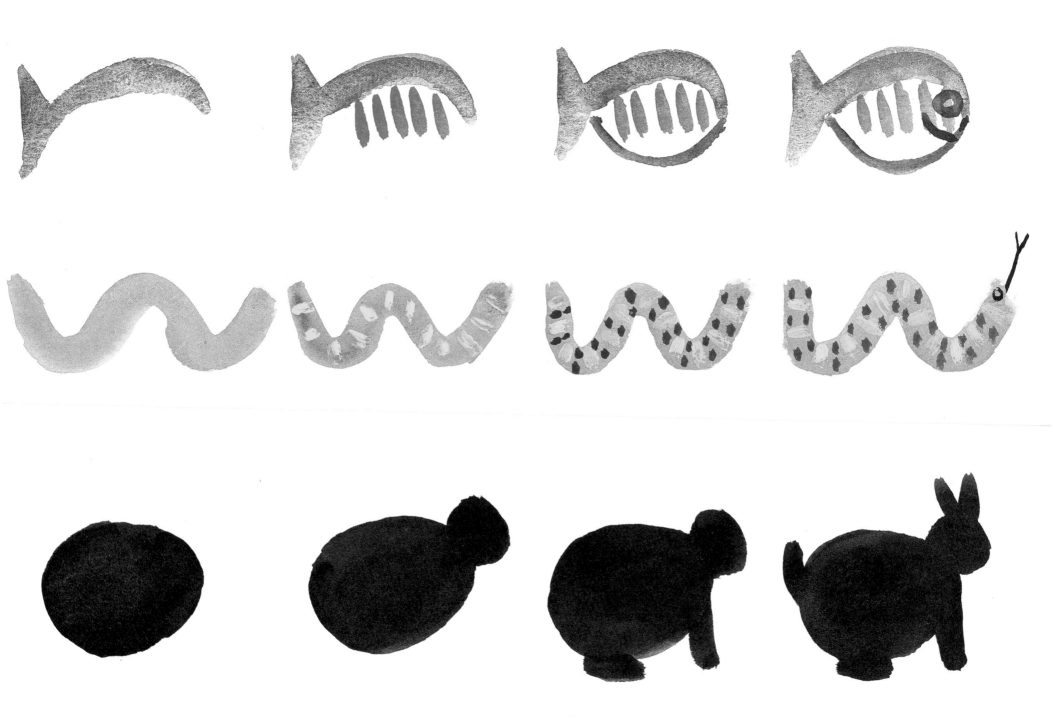

7 Daffy Ducks

These ducks will help you to learn about using lots of paint and very little water. That's the way to get really bright colors.

FIRST STEPS

Paint a half-circle in green paint. Don't put too much water on your brush, or the paint will be thin and runny. Add a little circle for the duck's head. Leave a little white space where the eye will be.

Remember that this paint is quite thick, so it may take an extra minute to dry. Add a dot of red for the eye, and paint in the yellow beak.

SECOND STEPS

Make a row of yellow ducklings by painting smaller half-circles.

Remember to keep the paint nice and thick, so the color is really bright.

THIRD STEPS

Paint a whole family of ducks and ducklings. Then add a line of wavy blue water for them to swim on.

8   Floating Flowers

These flowers are painted with lots of water and very little paint. This makes wonderful, swirly patterns that run into each other.

If you give the brush light pressure, the second color will begin to spread out and blend into the first.

FIRST STEPS

Draw lots of flower shapes with the pencil. Dip the thick brush into the water, and lift it straight out. Pick up a little color, and paint quickly over one whole shape. Don't try to make the color thick or even.

This time, don't wait until the paint is dry! Rinse the brush and pick up another color immediately. Add it to the center of the flower.

SECOND STEPS

Now do all the other shapes in the same way. Paint as fast as you can, so the first color is still wet when you add the second. Try using lots of pretty soft colors, just like flower petals.

This exciting idea is called painting *wet on wet*, and you can see why!

9   Cheerful Cows

What could be more cheerful than a herd of smiling cows?

FIRST STEPS

Start with the pencil, and draw a fat rectangle with rounded corners. Add a little oval at one side for the head. Mix a light brown color. Take a good brushful of clean water, then add a drop of red and a drop of blue. Try it on a scrap of paper. Paint in the cow's body. Let it dry.

Outline the head with black. Add the legs, and a tail with a tuft at the end. Outline the eyes, the ears (they stand out at the sides), a nice pair of horns – and a big smile!

SECOND STEPS

Now paint a row of baby calves. Start with a smaller rectangle.

Finish with a whole family, adding a few big black and brown spots.

10 Fantastic Fish

The sea is filled with brilliant fish. You can start with simple shapes, and use lots of bright colors.

FIRST STEPS

Begin by drawing circles and ovals in pencil. Add a little wedge at the back of each fish for the tail fin.

Pencil in the stripes, then paint the lines and stripes with the small brush, using black paint and very little water. Begin with the stripes which go up and down. Start at the front of the fish, and end with the tail. If you are left-handed, start with the tail. Then you won't smudge the paint.

SECOND STEPS

When the stripes run across the fish, start at the top and work down to the bottom. Remember to leave the eyes white. I didn't! Can you see which one?

Wash out your brush after painting each color.

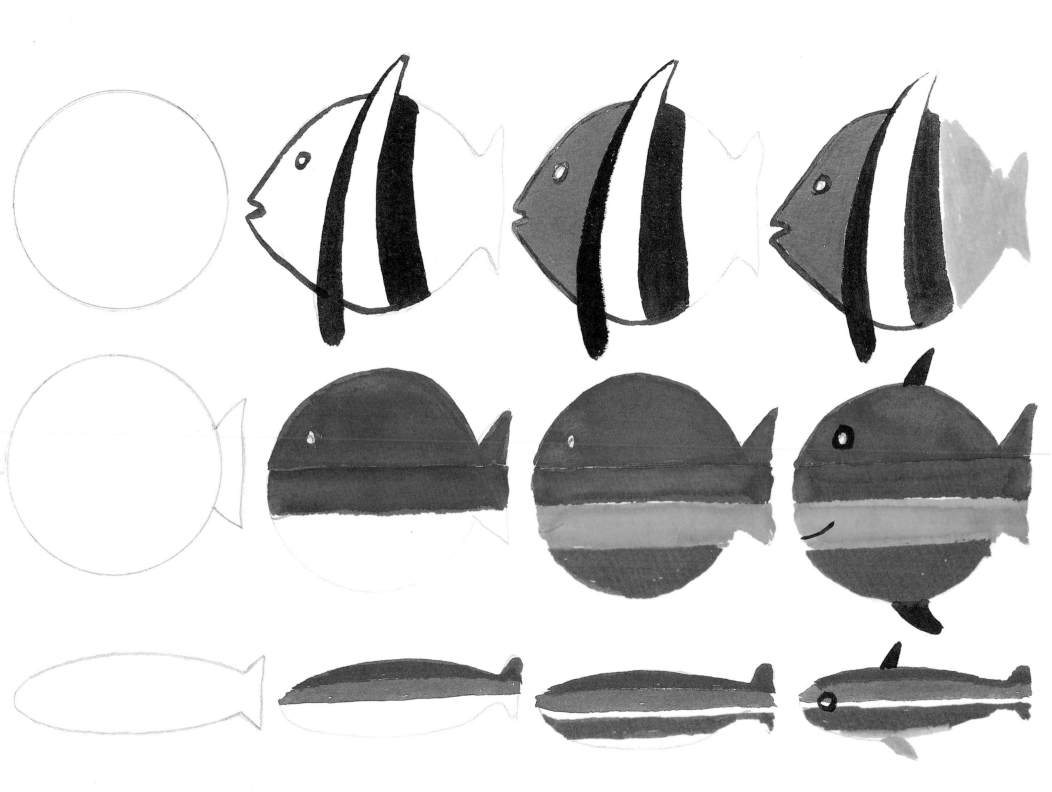

11   Outrageous Octopus

This friendly octopus is much easier to paint than you would imagine.

FIRST STEPS

Draw a simple oval in pencil. Add the bulging eyes, then give him a collar of eight fingers.

Now erase the ends of the fingers, so you have the beginnings of eight legs.

SECOND STEPS

Fill in the oval shape with red paint. Use the thick brush, and enough water to make the brush move easily and smoothly.

Now paint the legs. Sweep your brush from the top of each leg to a nice curve at the foot.

Add the lines and dots. Each round dot is a sucker which the octopus uses to pull himself along.

A real octopus is white or brown or grey, but I thought a red one would be much more cheerful and fun to do.

12   An Amazing Aquarium

Here's an aquarium where the fish and the octopus live.

Before you do anything else, make sure all the colors are really dry.

FIRST STEPS

Draw the aquarium outline. Put in circles and ovals for the fish. Add the octopus shape, and a curvy line at the bottom for the sand. Use the pencil lightly, so it's easy to erase and change things.

Paint the bright fish and the octopus. Mix light brown paint with a lot of water and a drop of red, then a drop of blue. Use it to paint the sand.

SECOND STEPS

Painting a background is something new. Use the big brush, plenty of water and just a touch of blue paint. Paint the top wave quickly, then brush across the page from top to bottom, circling around the fish and the octopus. Leave a little white around each one, so you don't cover their bright colors with blue.

Mix a light green color. Paint a few squiggly plants, then the glass around the aquarium.

13 Chirpy Chickens

Now you're going to paint all the animals you need for a picture of a farm. Chickens are absolutely essential to any farmyard, so we'll start with them.

FIRST STEPS

Draw the same shape that you used to make the ducks, only this time use the bottom half of the circle instead of the top half. Add a little circle for the head and then draw the neck. Remember to keep the pencil lines light so you can paint over them.

SECOND STEPS

Paint the body, and let it dry before you paint in the head and neck in a different color.

When both colors are dry, take the thin brush and add a few black lines for the feathers, the tail, the feet and the toes. Be very careful and make really narrow lines. If you have trouble, cheat a little and use a black pen until you can handle the brush.

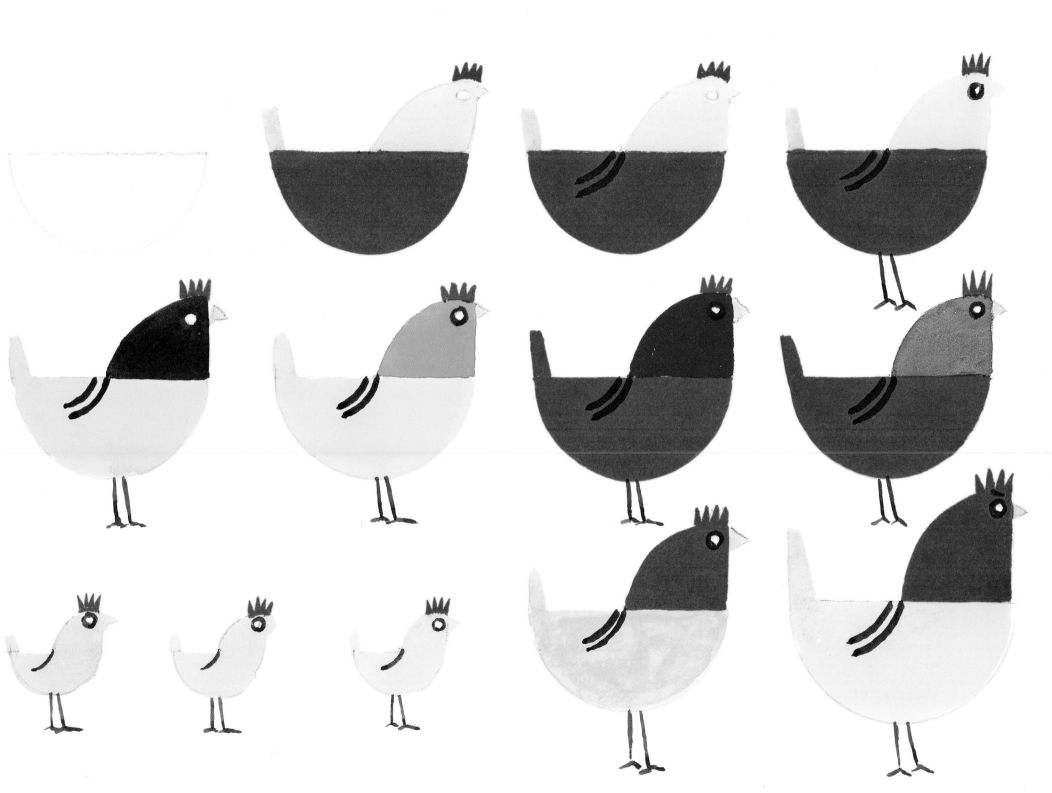

14 Perky Pigs

A happy family of perky playful pigs!

FIRST STEPS

Draw an oval for the body, then add the head, the ear pointing forward, the curly tail and the four little pointed legs. Erase the pencil so there is only a faint line to guide your paint.

Use the thin brush to paint round the whole pig with a dark pink, then use the thick brush to color in the pig's body with a lighter pink.

When the pink is absolutely dry, add the thin black line for the pig's smile and its eye.

SECOND STEPS

Draw in as many pink pigs as you like – the bottom row has a whole family!

Go over the pink carefully with black to add splashes and spots. What a perky paradise for playful pigs!

15 Lovely Lambs

Sheep have soft curls of wool all over their bodies – little curls for lambs, larger ones for sheep.

FIRST STEPS

Draw a rectangle lightly in pencil, then add the oval for the face and eyes. Remember the ears go out or down, not up like a cat or dog.

Take the thick brush, and fill in the bodies with black paint. Use very little water to get a really good color.

Paint around the eyes very carefully.

When the paint is dry, use the thin brush to add the ears, little skinny legs and tiny pointed hooves. Two round horns are a nice touch for some of the older sheep.

SECOND STEPS

The black sheep and the white sheep have a family of little grey lambs! If you add a drop of black to water, you can get a lovely shade of grey.

White lambs are hard to see on white paper! Try adding a little background – green grass, and blue sky around their heads.

16   Happy Houses

Houses come in many different shapes and sizes. Ours has curtains, a lovely red roof, and trees and bushes all around.

FIRST STEPS

Draw the outline of the house with your pencil, adding the windows and doors. Paint the walls, leaving white spaces where you are going to add different colors.

You may find it easier to use the thin brush for everything. Remember to wait until the walls are dry before you add anything else.

Paint the door, the curtains and the chimney.

Add the path, and use a little green paint for the front yard. Don't use too much water or the colors will run out of the tiny outlines.

SECOND STEPS

Why not paint a picture of your house, or your school? Paint your family in the yard, or your friends outside the school.

17   A Faraway Farm

This is a big project, so practice painting pigs, lambs, ducks and chickens before you begin. Use a big piece of paper or everything will have to be very small, and that is hard to do.

FIRST STEPS

Draw the whole farm in light pencil, including the oval pond. Make a tent shape for the chicken house. Draw in the fences, and the roads.

Start by painting the farmhouse. Remember to wait a minute and let each color dry before you add lines on top. Paint in the animals.

Remember their different sizes – a sheep is much larger than the chickens, which are about the same size as the ducks.

SECOND STEPS

For the sky, add a drop of blue paint to clear water. Add a little more blue to make the color of the pond.

Paint the fields and the roads. Use nice fat circles of green for the trees.

When everything is completely dry, draw in the fence lines carefully with black paint and a thin brush.

18   Crazy Colored Crocodiles

These are friendly crocs, in spite of their big teeth! Look at the smile on their long, long jaws.

FIRST STEPS

Draw lots of crocodile shapes in pencil first, adding bumps and humps just as you like. Just make sure each shape stays low and slithery.

Paint in the shapes in lots of bright colors. Make sure these are dry before you add anything else. Go around the big eyes carefully, leaving them white. Watercolor paints don't have a white; they let the white paper show.

SECOND STEPS

Add dots and stripes, squares and circles, squiggles and spots.

Use the thin brush to paint in the teeth in thin black lines. Outline the eyes in black too, and add the pupil right at the bottom.

In our croc family, the blue croc and the yellow croc have little green babies. This is to remind you that blue and yellow make green!

19 Weird and Wonderful

Now that you've learned how to make different shapes and how to paint with different colors, there is no limit to what you can put down on paper.

Draw every kind of shape you like. Add colors with lots of water or very little water.

Let the background colors dry and add patterns. Or keep them wet and add squiggles so they look like monsters left out in the rain too long!

When you are using so many colors, the water for rinsing your brush is bound to get dirty quickly. Remember to change the water whenever there is so much paint in it that you can't see through it any more.

20 At the End of the Day

All good artists take care of their materials, so they will last for a long time.

Start by putting your brushes in a glass of clean water. Leave them to soak while you tidy up.

If there are splashes on your paint box, clean them off now or they will melt into the color pans next time you start to paint. Take a very damp paper towel. Rub the splashes off gently. You can wash around the paint pans too, but be careful not to rub hard, or you will waste good paint.

Take the brushes out of the water and dry them gently with a clean bit of paper towel. Now throw the dirty towels away before you get paint on anything else!

Put the paint box carefully into a drawer, or on a shelf. Lay the clean brushes neatly alongside. If you have splashed the handles of the brushes, the pencil or the eraser, clean them before you put them away.

Rinse out the glass of water, and put it away.

Gather up your paintings – make sure they are

all completely dry before you put them on top of each other. Keep the best ones on one side to show what you have done.

Don't throw away any paintings, even the ones you don't like. Look at them and try to see what went wrong. Maybe you made the first outline too big, maybe you made it too small. Each picture should fill the page nicely.

Keep all your paintings for a while, so you can try and change things the next time you paint. Pin up the ones you like best! Everyone should have fun while they paint.

Being able to paint whatever you see and whatever you imagine – those are the first steps to being an artist.